to my LoverS

to my LoverS

Megan Parker

Moth to a Flame

to Jacy
to whom without, I would not be a writer

she also helped me curate the playlist that goes
along with the book
search "to my Lovers" on Spotify

everyone wants to find
their soulmate
but what do you do
when you find them?
do allow yourself to fall in love
with them?
what if they don't allow themselves
to love you back?
there are no stories about soulmates
that don't end up together
and are both still alive
expect for that one I wrote before

faith
(def)
an undeniable,
although sometimes wavering
belief in something magic
no matter the perception of others

we went from talking every day
even for just a little
to nothing at all
in that space of silence
I wrote letters to you every night
I can put words
to the hurt
that bleeds from my heart
that is what a good poet does
the pain in my heart had somewhere to go
a dream of the book
of the cover
of what I had to do next
then one day you were back
we were letting ourselves be friends again
but I was harbouring a secret
how could I not tell you?
how could I not leave it on your doorstep
and pray that you're the one to find it?

everyone in my life
has told me in some form or another
that I am too much
       too loud
       too intense
       that I need to calm down
       that I'm a show
I can change behaviours and patterns
but I cannot change who I am
what I am destined for
I am not afraid to speak up
       for what is important
       or for what I believe in
       or for those that don't have a voice
when I hear these things now
it is my cue

                        to be louder

I will find you in every life time
I have found you before
I will find you again
in this lifetime
I will find myself first

like the sun & the moon
they were fated to share the same sky
sometimes together, mostly not
the moments they came together
the whole world would come out
to witness their magic
an eclipse
is just a moment of oneness
but powerful enough for everyone to notice

like any good poet
I am alone
a victim to my heartbreak
struggling in love
tied to the sun and the moon
that is my muse
the Universe is yelling at me
      to not give up
      to believe
      to remember
it takes everything in me
to keep my faith

isn't it remarkable
that the whole Universe conspires
sometimes for years
for you to get the right message
at *exactly* the time you need it?

my last gifts to you
were a sunflower
for your birthday
along with a book that is filled
with words from my heart
that you called forth
I asked one last question
on that very last page
you are the only one who will ever see it
and only you can answer

I can feel when others read our story
I know you can too
their joy at our failure drains me
but the ones that have hope
the ones that our story resonates
they restore my energy
and my faith in our ending
they are the ones
that helped me start
a new chapter
knowing that this time
the ending
would be different
they are the ones that send me the song
that always makes me think of you
and send me moths
little ducks and baby chicks
fast cars
at the moment I need it

these memories of dreams
of actual moments
they soar in & out of me
like a hawk flying over head
I try to hold on to them
to remember them in detail
they are fleeting & slip through my fingers
because it is not me remembering
is it?

                                        it's you

you're reading it
the book I sent you
of my side of our story
when you read it
the memories flood back
exactly as they were
I am feeling your side now though
and have to apologize
for giving you doubt
thinking I was giving you space

I have a confession
I saved your confession
the one of reading front to back
with music
about how it made you feel
like you were there again

dream:
the moment you fell in love with me
was in the hot water
telling me the story
of tofu cooked in bacon fat
it was my laugh that did it
you fell in love with the sound
almost how
every time a bell rings
an angel gets it's wings

if I cannot see you now
in this world
than I will continue to ask
to see you in the other world
in my dreams
until they become real again

I thought the single
black glove was
a great move
until I realized how much
I wear those gloves
but not to worry
I find single black gloves
- serendipitously-
everywhere

I re-read
cover to cover often
each time
I see something different
your cover
I see your book
this secret project you
may or may not have
how it tastes
the stories within
and how you're smiling
with a red shirt on
a chef's hat in your hand
the constant need for more bookshelves
about how you and I will be co-captains
on our family ship
how it will finally feel to hold your hand
that I am our favourite poet
and it was my book that is worn

is what you saw that day on the mountain
was that you were wanting
for me to remember
who you really are?
or was it you realizing how much you missed me?
or were you remembering how it feels
when we are together?

dream:
your response about how you feel
you truly feel
in a book
that corresponds with mine

we are on a shelf with:
> Edward and Bella
> Hardin and Tessa
> Matthew and Diana
> Jamie and Claire
> Henry and Claire
> Garrett and Hannah
> Luke and Loreli
> Darcy and Elizabeth

my holding back
trying to honour
your boundary
fuelled
insecurity
doubt
you've been mad at me
since that night in the hot water
where I said you felt like home
the night where I should
have climbed into your lap
like we climbed the walls
looked into your eyes
and told you the truth

you let me fall in love with your light
what I am asking
is for a chance
to fall in love with your dark

it is not only time
that keeps me away
from you is it?
we are a run away train
rails don't seem much to matter
only a collision could stop us

even with you on one side of the ocean
& me on another
& a storm keeping us apart
I will sail until I see a light
& then I will wait there
until you find me
& I know you are safe

you will sail in your storm
I will sail in mine
until that day we meet
at the lighthouse again

you are always in my heart
but I wake every morning
dreaming of you
in my body

do you have any idea
how afraid
I am to feel everything?
what if after all this time
I get the chance
to fall in love with you
again

sunflowers
to me, you show up as sunflowers
I like to think that it is you sending them
to let me know
that you are thinking of me
as sign from the Universe
that is a gift from you

I want to stay in the world of the Spirit
where I don't make mistakes
where we are easily together
where everything is love

why is it that when
I am tired I am full
of second guessing
but as soon as I am in the forest
that guessing is gone
the trees help remind
me of who I am and what
it is I want

I'm really proud of myself
for not drunk texting you last night
because if I did
I would have admitted
that when you let your feelings out
and REALLY allow yourself to be you
your hugs are better

I had the most magical day
chasing waterfalls
not speaking a word
being in my own company
I waited for you
unknowingly setting a trap
that you fell into
when I watched you drive by
I've never let myself
cycle in that shame and anger
as much as I did that day
in my hardest drive ever
it took me six hours
of tears and feelings
to admit to myself
how afraid I am

you helped me realize
how much I fight
everything
I have been a warrior
for so long
fighting in a war for my heart
fighting for space
to be seen and heard
I have forgotten
that a warrior
is not who I am
it is only a part of me
after all these years of fighting
it is time to put the armour away

I have to stop
getting so mad at you
when you lie to me
I cannot command the truth
from you
or anyone
just like you
cannot command it
from me in
I don't always
want to speak
my truth to you
you should be
allowed
to lie to me
I should allow myself
to meet you
where you're at

even when the world
was ending
it was not enough
for you to say yes
and follow through

what do you think
the chances are
of me finding
every fictional book
that has to do
with soul-mates
-star-crossed lovers-
during a pandemic
where hand-held stories
are scarce?

I'll tell you

it's 100%

a decisive woman
who is independent
- self-sufficient -
is attractive at first
until you can't manipulate them
or change their mind
or talk them out of their decisions

Darcy.
your ass is definitely Darcy.

you're becoming
less and less prominent
in my thoughts
a ship sail from the shore
fade into the horizon
it was a whisper
a direction
I trust them
more than you
space and a wall
must be put up
not in anger
or as a result
because there were
steps I wasn't taking
waiting for you

it came up again
me being in your life
is stopping us both
from what we want
you know what you want
but it's not with me
I know what I want
and it's with you
but I am stopping myself from having it
afraid of your judgement
it is time to say goodbye
an electronic wall
a stop, a barricade, a block
I've held on for too long
I made the decision
immediately feeling lighter
while my brain screams
what have we done
while my gut and my soul sit silent, waiting
I am breaking a promise to you
and feel like I'm letting you down

giving up on you when I said I wouldn't
when everyone else has
I still have love for you
but I love myself more
my heart breaks
again
and not being able to say I'm sorry
I trust you to keep my most prized possessions safe
knowing that even if I never see you again
they are a small price to pay
for the time
and love I have for you
it feels like
giving up on you
but really
it's believing in me

dream:
your frustration at not being needed
at not being able to influence or manipulate
you think your opinion doesn't matter to me
it is part of your lesson
you see things
and I see things
my love,
you are wanted not needed
you would't want it to be any other way
I will always listen and hear you
but you need to learn
to be okay with me not always
following what you think is right
what you think and feel still matters
and it's your voice and heart that I need to hear
but we need to follow our own hearts
I will learn this with you too

I keep seeing visions
of you in the hospital
that I don't know what to do with
to either ask or tell
I can feel your heart hurting
even though I have no idea
where you are
I see flashes of worse case scenarios
deaths
you wishing I was there
but I'm trying to honour a promise
I made to myself
and not break it

why is it so hard
for me to allow
myself to be
in peaceful joy?
I have been practicing
being comfortable in calm
it isn't boring
or wasteful any more
it is content
I don't want to
leave it again
I don't want it to leave me

do you ever feel
like you want to go home
but you don't
actually know
what or where that is?

will there ever be a time
where a love story
doesn't trigger
thoughts of you?

you have no idea
how much I miss
talking to you
about absolutely nothing

a year
365 days
I've thought about you
on every single one of them
some days more than others
but I have yet
to miss a day

you're trying to get me to remember
to read the words in print again
to read the words here
        remember. remember
your energy whispers
the whisper is trying to change an outcome
because what I decided
doesn't suit you
and it's an outcome you didn't think would happen

there was a storm
beside a sunset
an evening of duality
an orb of glow
clouds edged, rimmed
with the strength of light
the darkness of the storm
the rip of lightning
the change of energy
they were not competing
they were holding space
for each other's power

I ask for it to fall on my lap
the one I'll feel safe with
for the Universe to bring them to me

I have done as much healing
as I can by myself
the next step is to do it with someone
there always is an opportunity for growth

what I get to ask for next
is to stop myself from fucking it up

seekers are curious
always after the truth and the story
they cannot be stopped
will constantly research
is it to validate truth
or to know more
I should not be surprised
that I attract them
moths
seekers seek the light

I wish it was you
but it's not
He's wonderful
but still not you
There is a different war within me now

How many people
-including fictional characters-
Can you be in love with
At the same time?
Asking for a friend

What scares me is not
If dating someone else
Doesn't work out
What scares me
Is dating someone else
and it does

I wake up thinking about
Someone else now
when I hear from you
the feelings aren't the same
they're.........quiet

He told me that I looked

Enchanting

As if I had been trying
To put a spell on him

He doesn't give a fuck
About who I am or what I do
He asks questions
Aware of his behaviours
He respects boundaries
He can receive
He can give
He is guarded but honest
He is calm but has desire
He is not afraid

Not yet

I'm dreaming of him
The life we once had
All the players in the game
Have finally arrived at the board

I lost the game
When we last
Were all playing
Pieces of ebony versus cream

In this life though
I am not a pawn
Something to be played
I will change the game

I am the Queen

My fingertips memorize faces
They trace the lines of the silhouette
Along the smooth length of a brow
They outline the lips
Subtly trying to coax out secrets
Finding hidden scars
Along strong jaws
Wounds from a war before

He leaves me with
My lips burning
My skin smelling of him
It distracts me from my sleep
As if my body is on fire
Tied to a stake
The dreams I keep
Having of him
Keep unfolding
Over and over
They're coming true
Feeling stronger and playing out in real life
It does not bode well

I feel the heat of
finding joy in another
the coolness of mourning
the true loss of you
it makes for the conditions
for a perfect storm
that I must weather alone
within me

He asked me what he tastes like
It's like when you lick your lips
After diving in the ocean
Like when you put your face
In the shower stream
He tastes like the
Element of water
Calm
Powerful
Restoring
Destructive
But I am an element of the earth

"Tell me what you want"

I asked, finally brave enough to be
Able to follow through
On his answer

"You" He whispered

He has yet
To make a wrong move
The old part of me
Doesn't trust the game
The part of me that's here now
Hesitates
Exposing my vulnerable side
The part I like the least
That is the only next move
It must be played
Not as a victim this time
From the strength of choice
As it is the only move
That I can play
If I want to win the game
This time around
In a game
That I don't want to play
Or even be in
It's time to do something
About it

There's starting to be
Grey area everywhere
A past life lesson
About choice
Always between people
Often between life or death
With my gifts
I can see the future
The choice that will
Have to be made
I will not put another
In that place of pain
It was time to be honest
Not prolonging another from meeting their soulmate
Which is what I am doing
If I hold on
Any longer

I've asked why

Why Him?
Why is he here again?

He has something of mine
A piece of my heart
From a long time ago
He is a Horcrux
A lesson in one step at a time
And betrayal
I asked permission
To look within my book
To see the contract
We both signed
For this lifetime

Forgiveness
Is the Lesson

There was a shift
A panic attack on the inside
It's riding a train all the way
To the station
Not knowing what is
Going to greet you there
When you arrive
Or if it is even safe for you
To do so
It's the realization that you are
On the wrong track
The wrong train
The wrong destination

How do you respond
To people that don't
Believe in magic?
You don't make it a point
To change their mind
You simply show them

Again
And again
And again

Until the proof is undeniable
They see the world within
Their hearts instead of their minds
Or
You leave them behind on your own quest
For someone who will respect your magic
And not burn you for it

He did everything right
Was delicious and wonderful
But a curse and blessing that comes with seeing
The future and know what will happen is just that
Ending something that hasn't begun
Because you know what will happen
Before it actually does
Which is really unfair for everyone
I won't see him any more
And I said goodbye to potential

Anyone that I am with
I cannot read or use my magic on
It makes me want them more
To understand them
Their patterns and their secrets
Which are readily accessible
For everyone else
It no doubt was a part of
Each contract
To make sure I was curious enough
To fall in love
With their puzzle

there is a hole in my heart
it grieves, the shape of you
it is angry at not letting
another be good enough
it holds on so tight
that it forces tears in others that I am teaching
it truly grieves for someone
who is not in this life
and another who is still alive
and realizing how much
I wrecked my own chance
at love

after another period of darkness
something happened today
a curl of a strangers hair
the way a boy called his girl 'babe'
a group of daisies
I am in love
but not with anyone
with life
there is more laughter
twinkling of eyes in the house
there is a shift
there is healing
I believe in the life I want to live
that finally, FINALLY
I am believing that I am worthy of it

I'm going to have to ask him
a big question
will you give up
your life for mine?
what I'm really going to be asking
is if you feel or believe
that I, me, is worth that sacrifice
that he will value me being different
handle me delicately because I'll be barely
holding it together
I imagine he'll ask me back

will you let me?

he will have to not only support me
but all the littles
while I support us

what's the deepest level
as to my want for someone?
it is the work
I want to share the work
not just Sunday breakfasts and laundry
but the work of family
of breaking patterns
the work of helping others
the work of choosing and taking care of each other
the work of love and joy
it is the work

believe me and in me
love me as much as I love them
want me as much as I want them
not be afraid of me and the life I want to lead
be fair, equal, open
ask me questions as much as I ask them
have crazy ideas
        lead
        listen
        speak
        understand
        believe
        support
able to flow with time
a want of big life too
never tell me that I am too much
able to hold space
intimate with their magic and alchemy
they need to be able to whisper "more"

a wish, dream, goal
what I want to learn is not
  only your body
  & what makes you groan
I want to learn your heart
  it's grief & joy
I want to learn your mind
  how you think & dream
  & words that form there
I want to spend the rest of my life
learning my favourite people
  you, me, our children, their partners, their children
  over & over
  every version
that is what I will learn in this lifetime

goldilocks zone
I think I have found
more of that sweet spot
where I'm content alone
not letting life pass me by
following my dreams
exploring the wants of my heart
not waiting
still wanting

dream:
a giant moth keeps visiting me
he has large eyes
that blink with curiosity
a hum that is healing
he feels very protective
with his cream and chocolate wings
that are the colour of your eyes
when they are in the light
the moths are finding me
they are in any light I am in
they follow me down paths
they find me alone in the night
others are sending them to me
I am a magnet
for their wings

the moths
I am seeing them again
I said before
that I would stop when the signs stopped
and I did
but now they're starting again
the little fuzzy birds too
which makes me wonder
what signs you are getting
and how your heart is doing?

there's this feeling
that haunts me today
I am sad because I feel lost
but I know who I am, my centre
it is not loss or sadness
it is missing of you
not the missing that comes
with the pain of grief
but the missing that comes
with the sound of your voice
a light that calls me home
that is what my heart hears with you
you have ruined me forever
in the best possible way

a repeating pattern
thiscloseto
hope
everything I wanted
tap tap
gone
it's happening again
a certain death
a lost key
& all I can think of
is you

it was always you
before I ever knew you were real
in this world and lifetime
it was always you
I don't want it to be you
it just IS you
there is no other way

double sided, bic pen
90s note folding
a triangle of power
I said what I wanted
I used your name
writing our lives together
it is a spell of sorts
my magic is in my words
both are powerful

a feeling that I had felt before
you were mine and I was yours
that pull on the heart
that feeling of home
it was familiar
the tree, the name
it was all lined up
I fought hard for it
I lost it
like I had lost you
I fought again
for what I felt was true
I fought until my heart broke
my tears & sadness
broke my wall
in defeat
I caved
it was the snow
and the time
an apology from my heart
a wish

dream:
you needed a ride to the airport
it's one of my favourite things to do, drive people
fill them with magic
before their adventure
you told me you were ready
at the departure gates
running in a different way
a safety net unless I didn't agree
it was mere weeks of back and forth
a different start
a new way of connecting
then I was ready by the time
I picked you up
this time at the arrivals gate

dream:
"you are my star"
is it you bringing me
these memories of you and I?
trying to remind me of what we had?
telling me that I am
a guiding light
that every star is a sun
and the centre of a universe?
something one orbits around
that feeds their very existence

dream:
you were on the train
I walked up behind you
you let me see your wings
my finger tips traced
the hard lines and left smudges
your wings were't grey but white
you had never let anyone
help you clean the hard work off of them

I remembered this walking in the woods
on a windy day
where I could feel my wings
stretch and unfurl, remembering
that they could be full
as the wind shook the dust from them
the light shone upon my face
I felt my heart pull tighter together that day
as the phoenix within me, rose again

the dream keeps
coming back
the one where we
go bungee jumping
tied together
dangling from a bridge
you whisper to me
"let go"
I can't
I am afraid of how much it hurts
but when I dream of it now
we're holding hands
letting go together
with smiles in our eyes

dream:
it's the first night
in a new house
spaghetti
on the menu
knock knock
it is you
and your little
just in time
for dinner
you stay
fleeting moments
watching a movie
starting small
there is space
ease
laughter
for all of us
dinner is ready
and so am I

anxiety woke me from sleep
a tiredness had seeped into my bones
and my lungs
viral
energy woke me
yours
at the front door
six feet away
gifts, food and well-wishes
sunshine and socks
I couldn't breathe
or focus
you felt nervous
you looked good
your energy was different
grown
you felt......you felt...... ready
I had to ask if it was real
it wasn't a dream this time

a conversation
about pasta and dairy
that feels like
a fresh start
sunflowers, all the sunflowers

the last time I left seeing you
I gave the Universe specific instructions, boundaries
that would need to be followed
in order to give my heart
permission to try with you again
you asked me to do all of them
down to the T

I want to wrap
my hands around it
protect it
from outside judgement
prying eyes
other's influence
this small flame
that's you and I
starting again
you're trying to get me
to give it more air
have us breathe together
for everyone to see & hear
just a while longer
it will never be
just you & I again
it is precious
this glowing ember

a feather in my bath water
floats in broken tension on the surface
my sadness with you now feels hopeful
I am glad to have it
it feels delicate
like a feather on bath water
it could stay there until the flow is gone
or it could drown

I love when you send me pictures
I love to see the way
you see your every day world
and want to share it with me
it's really hot
when you trust me enough
to let me in

will you take me to see the stars?
to that place where we can put
our toes in the sand?
with the shadow
of the chalice
of the Earth
that cradles the Milky Way
and the night sky?

a kiss on the cheek
the top of the head
the tip of the nose
all add up to
catching feelings
a pull
from the depths within
that only your magic
has ever reached
I bite my lip as the butterflies
within me converse
to be nervous or excited
as your energy is drawing them
to the next steps
they decide to be both
as my heart allows

the string between us
it pulls tighter
pulling us together
it pulls on both of us
& keeps us up at night
it will not break

every thing we did
that afternoon
was illegal
every moment
was worth
the rebellion
you taste like snowflakes
that melt on my tongue
you taste like magic
you wore a red shirt
holding hands
sunset on the bench
the snow as company

there's a certain way
that hands are placed
across one's back
that all mean something different
your hands
against my lower back
pushed my body
as close as you dared to yours
things are starting
to line up

one day
soon
we won't have to hold back
or stop
but simply
let go
& enjoy
savour
each other
like we've been supposed to
this whole time
in every area
of life

hours again
it felt like the top of the world
white & grey
trees breaking the skyline
a crow afar
your arm around me
it was silent
calm
the world at peace
all the thinking for both of us stops
in that quiet
they are stitching us together
there is relief in the feeling
welcoming the feeling
a breath out
of no longer having to stop
but simply enjoy the company
of each other

I'm falling asleep
with your words
in my heart

patience
teaching a new skill
15-2
15-4
a pair is 6
a new way for me to use cards
a need to learn
so we can play together always
even though
your count is immediate

there is always two of us
there is the one that is here
      in a physical body, burning
there is another
      that is used to being hidden
      energy, a flame
they both meet
as your hands hold my face
as you kiss me again
giving fuel to the fire
it is getting harder to stop
to control
to walk away
from the fire that threats to consume
how I will not stop it
but welcome it
with an open heart

"give me something to write about"
a poet demands, lips upon lover's lips
he took her hands
pinned her against the wall
and she let him take her words away

I hope you know
how much I have missed you

since when?

since always

feeling
each time deeper
it's harder to go
to stop
to pull away
to leave
I am falling deeper
drowning in what I feel
having to practice
letting myself
allow it to happen

glass slippers
ice cleats
whatever you call them
you were my Prince to put them on
making sure that they fit
and that I was safe

down into the canyon
sunlight throwing fire on the mountain tops
the forest quiet
waiting
the river coursed beneath the ice
it's power pulsing
waterfalls frozen into icicles
to climb behind
to experience
to breathe in
to feel
to be
an alcove
a frozen spot of the water to fall
we lay on a blanket
laying to watch the sky
the frost from the fall
swaying in the wind
a mirror to the kelp that sways in the current of salt water
there was a thin veil
between reality and energy

were we at the base of the falls?
or at the bottom of the ocean?
it was another world
another time
another life
but it was now
and your warmth was an anchor
to what really mattered

somehow the view of the mountains
gets even better
when you wrap your arms around me
from behind
permission to do that
for the rest of our lives
to all the vistas and views
that we will have from the windows
of our home and of travel
the perfect day
the one with the new crown
ended with that kiss to end all kisses
you holding onto me
as my knees gave out
there were no jokes about swooning this time
your lips made me do it

gratitude
appreciation
communication
openness
trust
quality time
respect
compassion
understanding
truth
it's the work
you & I both know
how important it is

I can no longer tell
if it is you or I
that think 'I love you'
I can feel them to slip into my mind
and want out of my mouth
is it you or I?
I can no longer tell
and it no longer matters

don't do that - don't leave
you waited a year and a half for me,
now I can wait a while for you

one day
there won't be an alarm to leave
there will be a space for us to be
there will be a start, for all of us
no more maybes

the moment
you demand the moment
the quiet
to let go
      mountains & waterfalls
      the ocean
      the forest
      the sun
      the moon
      the stars
all demand the same
the moment
it is what I surrender too

ssshhhhh
you whisper
hush
into my mouth
as your lips
& your hands
control the moment
it was so quiet
all there was
was touch

your fingertips
ignite a deep energy
within me
that has been dormant
this whole lifetime
your fingertips
call it to the surface
causing me to writhe
against you
as I lose control
your fingertips
they control me
you are an artist
painting with fire
that burns inside me
bringing it out
for us both to see

the mornings of me waking up alone
are numbered and drawing to an end
I think of the ways that we will wake
each other up now when my eyes open
little spoon
big spoon
a tangle of legs
fingertips tracing shoulders and spines
a kiss on the neck
tucking into arms
hands tangles in hair
always our hands
come together
when they do, I open my eyes
but instead of my words to describe it
there are your words of your heart
that I wake up to

it snows just for us
it blesses our eyelashes & tongues
the same as the love around us
it is growing
can you feel it?
you can
because you spent a day
making me a representation
you can feel the life within it
it's wings beat as my heart does

"can I share something with you?"
a question before you sent me
words of your own
that you had written
- fairly recently -
inspired from
something I have yet to hear about
I waited
now you wait
for our time together
to tell stories
answer questions
to start and end each day
with your lips upon mine
with all of our hearts
under the same roof

I understand now
why it is getting so hard to
leave your side
there have been too many
lifetimes where I have
not been able to
I am afraid
that now that I have you
and you have me
that we will once again
have a life
with no chance
to say goodbye

it's those tiny moments
a kiss before going into the post office
taking my tea bag out of my mug
me cheating at a game
changing my socks for me
it's those tiny moments
that I saw us old together doing
but I only experienced them once
now it will be my memories
that grow old with me
instead of you
how quickly
it can all change

I dream of your lips upon mine
of not needing to leave or to stay
of thinking that I had found it too
in a moment the winds changed, and you were gone
without a real chance to say good bye
like all those lifetimes before

Grandmother Willow asks, "do you trust him?"
yes

She asks again, "do you love him?"
yes

"then what else is there, child?"

there is the Truth

you gave me an incredible gift
my own value
on a day
where you questioned mine
not just questioned
but argued
angry
not only at what I do
but how I do it
what I exchange for energy
how you think it should be done
instead of trusting me
you compared my worth to others
one's you feel are more deserving than mine
strangers who's worth you value more
you've never even seen what I can do
you've never truly felt my work
you don't know what I can do or what I've done
how I serve others
you ended things over something
that is intangible

something that you said you didn't care about
that I said I didn't care about
you gave more power over a number
than you did how you felt
this was a different kind of heart break
as you saw me beneath not only you
but others
I took my value back that day
I hate that it was you that gave me the lesson
I love that it was you that gave me the lesson
I forgive that it was you that gave me the lesson

pull
pulling at a thread
unraveling
revealing
there is more to the story
it goes further back
that first time
crossing paths
a year before, before
where the strings were short
how many times
will fate cross our paths?
how many times
will we keep getting in our way
how many times more
will you regret
not following the string
that connects
your heart to mine
this red string of fate
is the weaver of our story

I am the wind
that brings the gifts
in the rain & the snow
that moves to the branches
& flips the leaves
I am the wind
that changes the energy
but is not predictable
I am the wind
that comes with change
& moves on

I settled for the sun
to be the one to comfort me
to kiss my neck
in an attempt to remind me
that I am not alone
I crave to read your words
like I crave your touch
and to hear your voice again
I crave it like how I want to
> throw rocks in a still pond
> or jump into an empty pool
> or fall upon fresh snow
> or crack the ice upon a puddle
it is a temptation I do not stop myself
from following through
I do not stop until content
I find that I am
not a victim of love
when I have taken the time
to nourish my soul

Lightning Source UK Ltd.
Milton Keynes UK
UKHW020640270922
409514UK00009B/540